THE POCKET

OP ART

Published in 2025
by Gemini Books
Part of Gemini Books Group

Based in Woodbridge and London

Marine House, Tide Mill Way,
Woodbridge, Suffolk IP12 1AP
United Kingdom

www.geminibooks.com

Cover illustration by Natalie Foss

ISBN 978-1-80247-287-5

Printed in China

10 9 8 7 6 5 4 3 2 1

MIX
Paper | Supporting
responsible forestry
FSC® C020056

Picture credits: Associated Press / Alamy Stock Photo 20. Getty Images:
Jack Mitchell 34, 44; Raphael Gaillarde 58; Emiliano Lasalvia 104. Ph "Il
Maestro Getulio Alviani" 82. Special thanks to Valeria Gennuso, "Getulio
Alviani archive and research study center" 92. Courtesy of the artist's
estate and Locks Gallery 114. Courtesy of the Stanczak Foundation 70.
Image © Tatsuo Kondō. Courtesy D. Wigmore Fine Art, Inc. 122.

THE POCKET

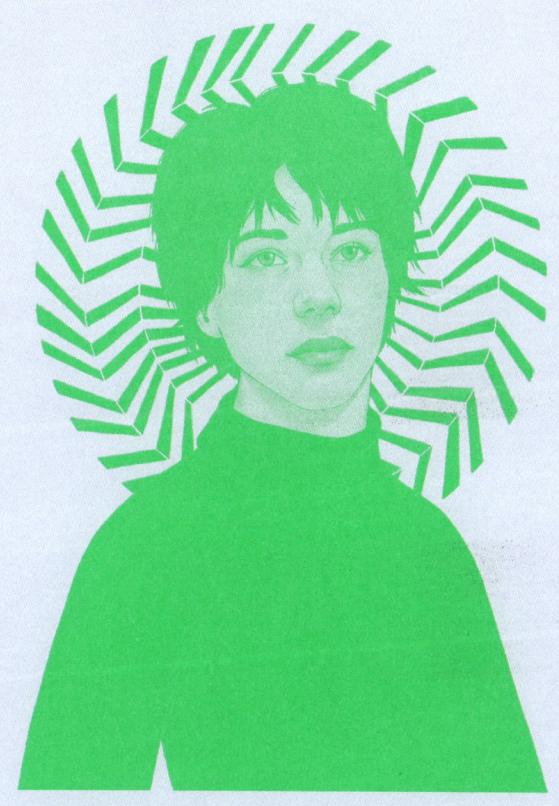

OP ART

G:

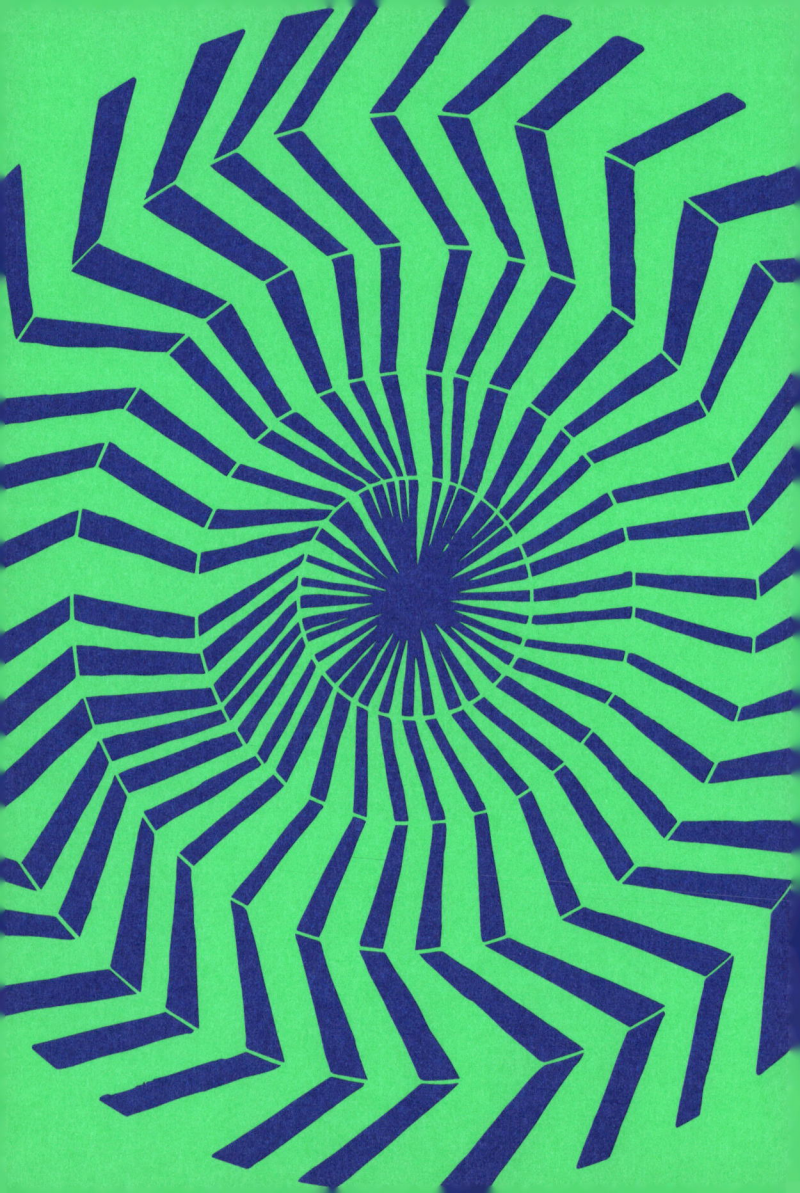

CONTENTS

INTRODUCTION

Op Art will trick your eyes! Using optical illusions, it will make your mind shift and your vision vibrate. Short for "optical art", the movement emerged in the 1960s and was all about using geometric patterns, shapes and colours to create movement and depth. Today, its influence is everywhere, in fashion, music and advertising, while its artists are celebrated for their visionary approach to the experience of art.

This pocket guide presents some of the leading lights of the movement – from Bridget Riley, and Victor Vasarely to Julian Stanczak and Jesús Rafael Soto – looking at their work, influences, connections and their thoughts. As Op Art's key figures, they stand the test of time, keeping it real with their radical art that explores how we see the world around us.

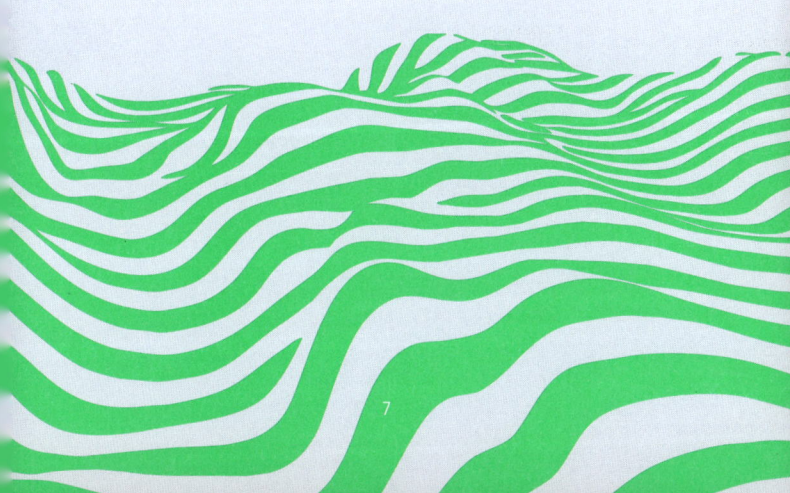

ORIGINS & INFLUENCES

WHAT IS OP ART?

Op Art was an abstract art movement that came to prominence in the 1960s, which made use of geometric forms, patterns, light and colour to create images that give the illusion of movement.

Short for "optical art", the phrase was first used in 1964, when artist Donald Judd reviewed Julian Stanczak's Optical Paintings exhibition in New York. It relates to how the human eye perceives certain types of two-dimensional (2D) artwork – most notably repeated forms and patterns – and "sees" motion, distortion and an illusion of three-dimensional (3D) space.

MOVING PARTS

Op Art is often discussed in relation to kinetic art, as both share a fascination with movement. However, while kinetic art features real motion – its artworks often take the form of mobiles or sculptures with moving parts – Op Art creates this illusion through its arrangement of shapes and colour on a canvas. Some leading op artists also made kinetic art and vice versa, notably Jesús Rafael Soto and Julio Le Parc.

ORIGINS

Op artists were influenced by a wide range of modernist movements, including the late 19th and early 20th-century movements of post-impressionism, cubism, futurism and constructivism. All these styles contributed to the wealth of modernist art movements that developed, waxed and waned during the 20th century, overlapping and influencing each other and having a profound effect on emerging artists in the post-war period.

"The purpose of my work is to help the person who looks at it to realize a perception of the whole universe as an endless, visually perceivable entity."

VICTOR VASARELY,
THEBOOKEY.APP

NEW WAYS OF SEEING

Post-impressionists, such as Cézanne and Van Gogh, had reacted against realistic depiction of detail in art in favour of exploring colour, line and form. In turn, the post-impressionists influenced the revolutionary movement of cubism, which saw Picasso and Braque, among others, bring multiple views of their subjects together in the same picture. This produced paintings that looked fragmented – somewhat like a broken mirror – and increasingly abstract in nature.

Around the same time, futurism, originating in Italy, was also rejecting traditional forms of art, embracing the dynamism of the modern world and its new technologies. Constructivism, coming from Russia, took this a step further, with its use of stark, abstract, structural forms that reflected the industrial world.

Such movements had laid the groundwork for Op Art, which came to prominence in the 1960s. Its earliest example is often cited as *Zebra*, which was painted in 1937 by Victor Vasarely. Known as the "grandfather" of Op Art, Vasarely used black and white stripes with no outlines to show two intertwined zebras on a black background. The movement in *Zebra* foreshadows the intense optical effects of later Op Art, and Vasarely – along with British artist Bridget Riley – became its best-known exponent.

THE RESPONSIVE EYE

Op Art was put firmly on the map
when the Museum of Modern Art
(MoMA) in New York opened an
exhibition called The Responsive
Eye in February 1965. Featuring
more than 120 pieces by a wide range
of artists, the exhibition was hugely
popular with the public and went
on to tour several cities in the USA.
Critics were less kind, however,
defining the movement as more an
act of trickery than a presentation of
serious art.

While some artists expressed regret about the subsequent commercialism of Op Art that came out of the exhibition, its main purpose had been to provoke discussion about the nature of seeing – a process that involves the brain and nervous system of each individual participant and therefore elicits different responses. Influential artist and art teacher Josef Albers, who also had several pieces on display, taught that "art is not object, but experience", and this principle certainly held true for Op Art and other immersive art forms that followed it.

"Focusing isn't just an optical activity, it is also a mental one. It is important that the painting can be inhabited, so that the mind's eye, or the eye's mind, can move about it credibly."

BRIDGET RILEY,
THE EYE'S MIND: BRIDGET RILEY COLLECTED WRITINGS 1965–1999 BY ROBERT KUDIELKA, 1999

POPULAR APPEAL

Despite some of the criticism attracted
by the MoMA exhibition, it made great
successes of many of the artists involved.
They became in demand internationally and
their work widely exhibited. Many famous
Op Art pieces became widely reproduced in
popular culture, especially fashion and music,
albeit often without the permission of their
creators. The op artists themselves continued
to explore their art of perception, going on
to develop it individually in a variety of ways,
and their work is still popular today.

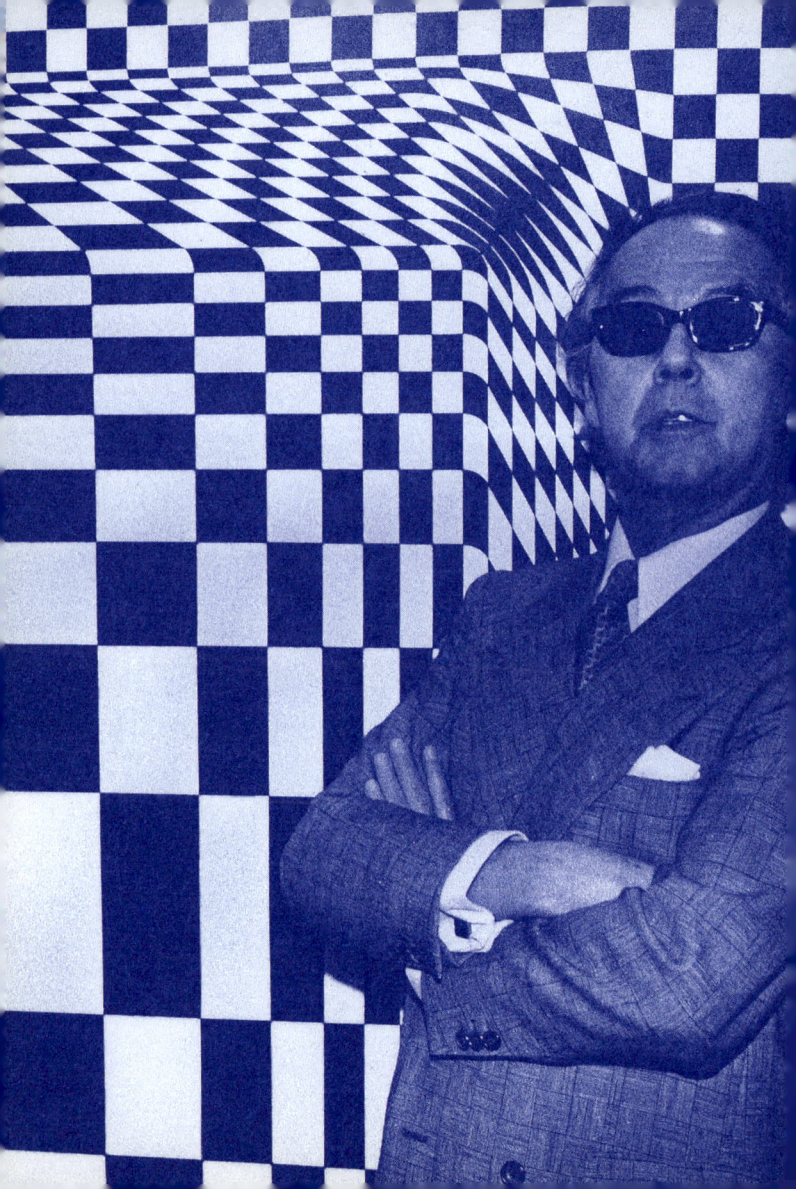

VICTOR VASARELY

1906–1997

Place of birth/death:
Pécs, Hungary/Paris, France

Key works:
Zebra (1937)
Tribute to Malevitch (1954)
Kalota (1963)
Orion MC (1964)
Vega-Nor (1969)
Vega 200 (1968)
Banya (1964)

EARLY YEARS

Credited as the visionary who created the Op Art movement, Hungarian-born Victor Vasarely first studied medicine in Budapest before switching to art school in 1928. He married and moved to Paris in 1930, and was based in France for the rest of his life. Vasarely's early interest in science as well as art helped define his creative vision. He maintained an intense fascination with what the eye perceives, and the language of seeing, throughout his long artistic career.

Vasarely worked as a graphic designer in advertising agencies to support his young family, one of whom – Jean-Pierre Yvaral – would go on to become an op artist himself. Working in advertising gave Vasarely an insight into how people respond to images and process visual information. This, combined with an interest in graphics and geometric patterns, influenced his art from his earliest 1930s' works onwards.

"My aim is to show that we perceive reality from different points of view, that with each individual's perception, the world is subjected to infinite changes."

VICTOR VASARELY,
THEARTSTORY.ORG

ZEBRA

BY VICTOR VASARELY, 1937

Location: Pompidou Center, Paris, France

From the beginning, Vasarely's art plays with perception and his 1935 *Chess Board* and 1937 *Zebra* were two graphic monochrome pieces featuring objects he would return to repeatedly in later years. *Zebra*, often cited as the first Op Art painting, presented black and white wavy lines on a black background to show two overlapping zebras in a way that is unsettling and disorientating to the eye the more one looks at it.

DEFINING A MOVEMENT

Vasarely continued to develop his talents throughout the 1940s and 1950s, holding his first solo exhibition in an avant-garde gallery in Paris in 1944. Influenced by artists such as Wassily Kandinsky and Paul Klee, and the movements of cubism, futurism, constructivism and suprematism, he experimented with paintings, collage and sculpture, finding his own style of abstract art with its geometric but fluid forms.

In the summer of 1948, Vasarely spent time in the small French town of Gordes in Provence, where he found that working in the bright sunshine sometimes played tricks on his eyes, with solid objects and sharp shadows becoming confused and interchangeable. He wrote, "Thus identifiable things are transmuted into abstractions and begin their own independent life."

ART FOR ALL

Over the following decade,
Vasarely began to sharpen his ideas
and direction into what would
become known as Op Art. He
also experimented with kinetic
art and large-scale murals, such as
1954's *Tribute to Malevitch*, a 330-foot
(100-metre) square ceramic-tiled wall
piece that adorns the University of
Caracas in Venezuela. This fitted
well with his slogan, "art for all", and
his desire to see his work outside
galleries and in public spaces.

"Geometry
in my paintings
is the source
of a universe
that takes life
through colours."

VICTOR VASARELY,
THEARTSTORY.ORG

MOMA RULES

Vasarely had six pieces on display at MoMA's 1965 The Responsive Eye exhibition, including *Orion MC* (1964) and *Kalota* (1963), both colourful artworks of a variety of repeated geometric patterns. He was interested in the language of colour and often produced similar works in a range of palettes.

Following the success of this exhibition, Vasarely's art continued to grow in popularity, with his *Vega* series becoming his best-known work. An early example is 1957's *Vega*, a black and white chequerboard of different squares and quadrilaterals, that gives the effect of spherical shapes pushing into and out of the canvas. Later *Vega* works employed similar effects showing a large ball that seems to swell through a grid of coloured circles towards the viewer.

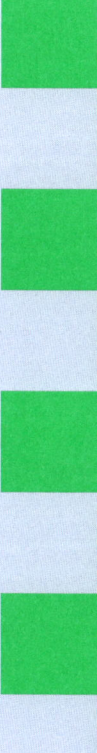

OUT OF THIS WORLD

Perhaps befitting a modernist artist who applied a scientific approach to his work, Vasarely was fascinated by the space race that captivated the world from the late 1950s and through the following decade into the 1970s. Works from this period were named after stars, planets and galactical events, with their shimmering optical effects reflecting the wonders of the space age. His fame reached beyond the art world too, with a Vasarely design being used as background art for the cover of David Bowie's eponymous second album in 1969. And in 1982, a French astronaut took 154 specially created Vasarely prints on a mission to the Salyut 7 Soviet space station. These "out of this world" artworks were later sold for charity.

LEGACY

By the time of his death in 1997, aged 90, Vasarely had been awarded multiple international art prizes, held more than 150 solo exhibitions worldwide and had two museums dedicated to his work. One is in his birthplace of Pécs, Hungary, and the other in Aix-en-Provence where the Fondation Vasarely continues to preserve his work and legacy.

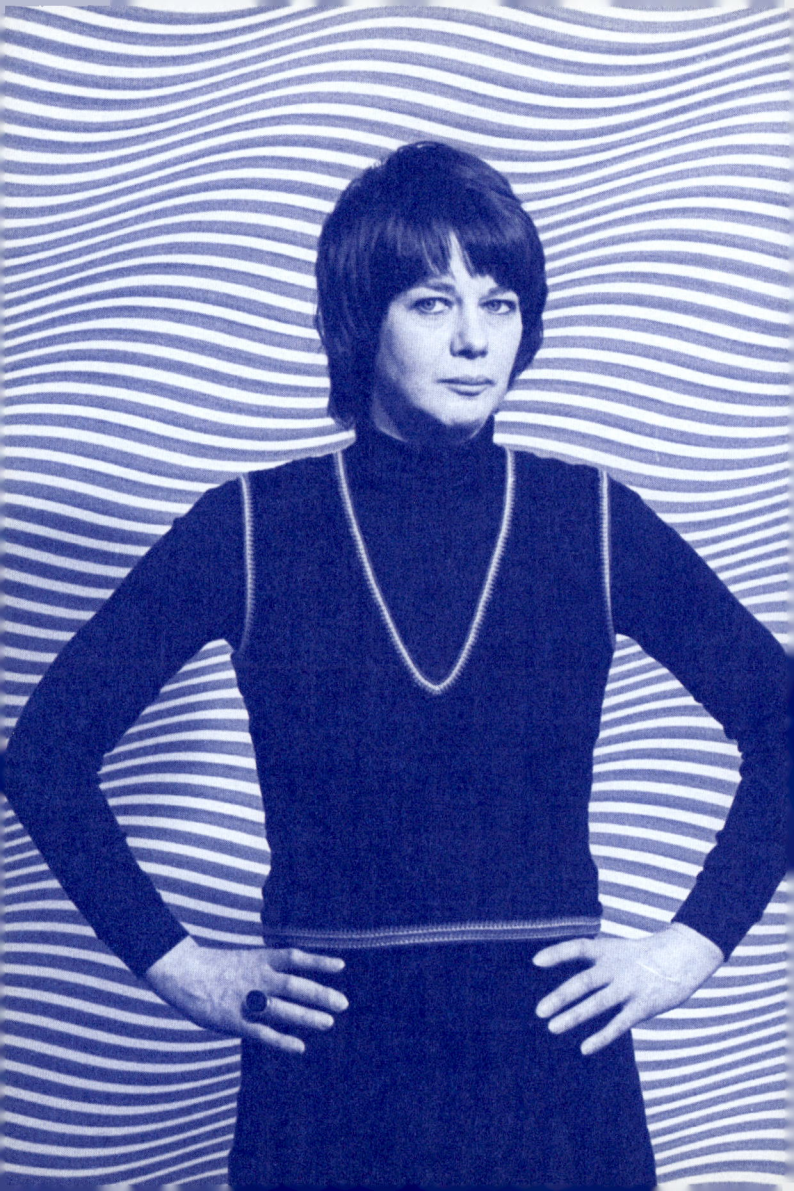

BRIDGET RILEY

1931–

Place of birth:

London, England

Key works:

Kiss (1961)
Movement in Squares (1961)
Blaze (1964)
Current (1964)
Cataract 3 (1967)
Cantus Firmus (1972–73)
Achaean (1981)

EARLY YEARS

Born in London in 1931, Bridget Riley moved with her mother and sister to live with her aunt in Cornwall during the Second World War. Riley's aunt introduced her to art, and the scenic surroundings of her wartime home became her earliest artistic inspiration. "There was nothing to do but look and enjoy and appreciate... this extraordinarily beautiful landscape," she later recalled.

After the war, Riley studied at Goldsmiths College and the Royal College of Art before working as an art teacher and as an illustrator for a London advertising agency. Her early work was figurative but as her art matured, she was influenced in particular by French neo-impressionist Georges Seurat and his pointillist style of painting. Pointillism used small separate dots of colour to make up a recognizable image, and Riley made her own copy of Seurat's *The Bridge at Courbevoie*, using it as inspiration for her own exploration of the different ways the eye "sees" art.

"There was a time
when meanings were
focused and reality
could be fixed;
when that sort of
belief disappeared,
things became
uncertain and open
to interpretation."

BRIDGET RILEY,
THEARTSTORY.ORG

FIRST ABSTRACTIONS

Riley developed her abstract optical style in the 1960s, having her first solo exhibition in London in 1962. Her early works were mostly black and white geometric paintings which demanded active participation from the viewer with their disorientating sensations of movement. Examples include *Movement in Squares* (1961), and another well-known Riley piece from this period, *Current* (1964), with its close black and white wavy lines. *Current* graced the cover of MoMA's catalogue for its infamous 1965 exhibition, The Responsive Eye.

By the end of the 1960s, Riley had started to introduce colour into her work, notably in 1967's *Cataract 3*, where fine coloured stripes are presented in curvilinear waves across the canvas to challenge the eye and give a distinctly 3D effect. In 1968, she was the first woman to win the International Prize for Painting at the Venice Biennale.

MOVEMENT IN SQUARES

BY BRIDGET RILEY, 1961

Location: Arts Council Collection, London, England

Riley's first major Op Art painting, *Movement in Squares* (1961), features a chequerboard of black and white squares that decrease in width to an off-centre point, drawing the viewer into the work and giving the effect of movement. This play of distortion and rhythm gives the work a kinetic energy, even though it is entirely static.

"For me nature is not landscape, but the dynamism of visual forces. These forces can only be tackled by treating colour and form as ultimate identities, freeing them from all descriptive or functional roles."

BRIDGET RILEY, *THE EYE'S MIND: BRIDGET RILEY COLLECTED WRITINGS 1965–1999* BY ROBERT KUDIELKA, 1999

BEYOND MAGIC

As the Op Art movement ebbed, Riley continued her bold, abstract style in subsequent decades, using brilliant colours and repeated shapes in her unending study of perception. In later years, she also became known for her large-scale murals in public spaces. These included applying bold, colourful stripes to the walls across three floors in St Mary's Hospital, London, in 1987 and 2019, with a view to lifting the spirits of staff and patients.

Still working today, Riley is one of Britain's most respected artists, with her art hanging in galleries worldwide, and several major cities, including London and Edinburgh, hosting retrospectives of her work. While her Op Art paintings might appear magical as the eye gazes at them, they are not simply optical tricks but a keen exploration of colour, light and form in a pure abstract style that she has made her life's work.

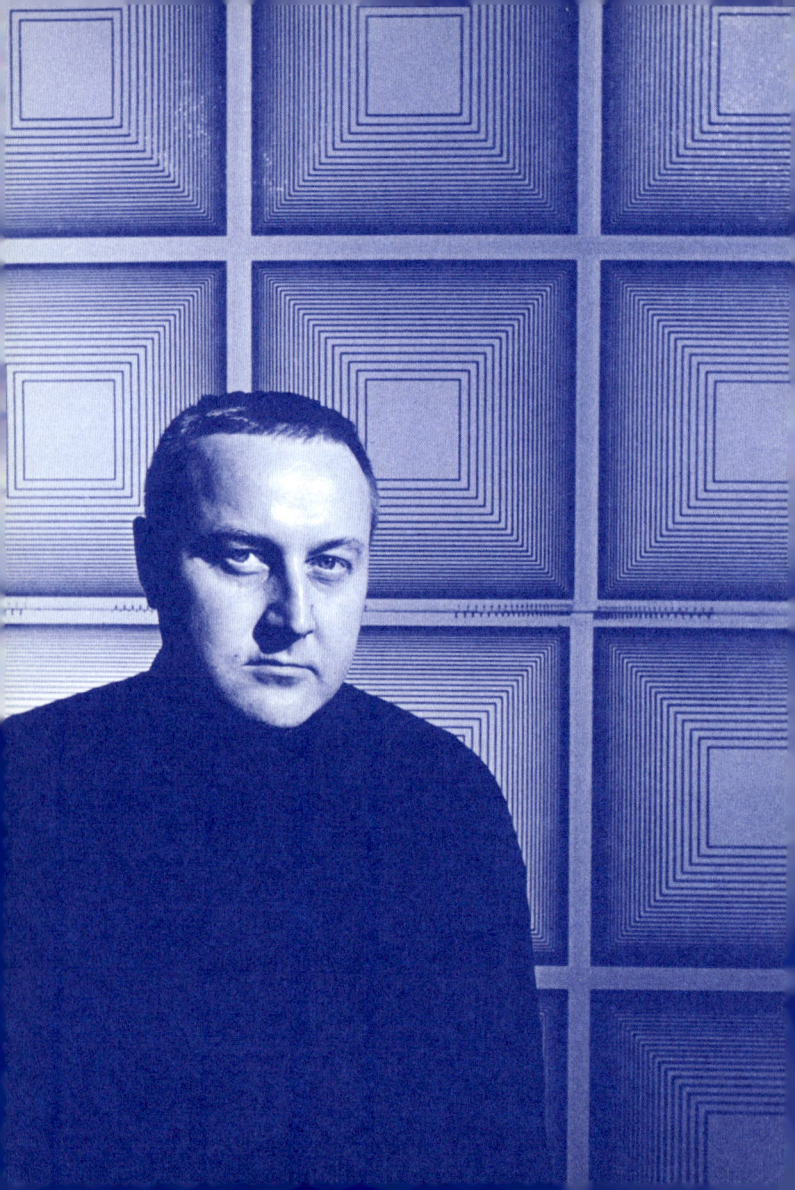

RICHARD ANUSZKIEWICZ

1930–2010

Place of birth/death:

Pennsylvania, USA/New Jersey, USA

Key works:

Fluorescent Complement (1960)
Knowledge and Disappearance (1961)
All Things Do Live in the Three (1963)
Sol I (1965)
Magenta Squared (1969)
Temple of Midnight Red (1983)
Translumina Trinity II (1986)
Translumina-Marriage of Silver and Gold (1992)

EARLY YEARS

American op artist, Richard
Anuszkiewicz, was born in
Pennsylvania in 1930. The son of
Polish immigrants, he studied at the
Cleveland Institute of Art and Yale
School of Art, where he roomed with
fellow op artist Julian Stanczak and
graduated with a Master's in 1955.

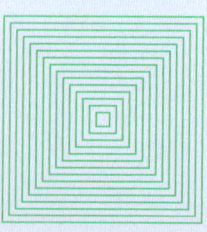

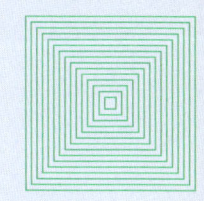

"Geometry and colour represent to me an idealized classical place that's very clear and very pure."

RICHARD ANUSZKIEWICZ,
ARTNET.COM

THE BAUHAUS EFFECT

Both Anuszkiewiez and Stanczak were taught by the influential art teacher and artist, Josef Albers, who inspired a generation of American abstract artists. Albers, who was born in Germany, had studied and then taught at the famous Bauhaus school between 1920 and 1933, when the Nazis shut it down. He moved to America to teach and became well known for his work on colour theory. The influence of his teaching and some of his art can clearly be seen in Anuszkiewiez's work, with its use of strong complementary and contrasting colours to create unusual visual effects.

Anuszkiewicz admired constructivism, with its simple, structural abstract forms, and also drew inspiration from artists such as Paul Klee and Wassily Kandinsky, both abstract pioneers who had taught at the Bauhaus and had a deep interest in colour theory. Along with Stanczak, Anuszkiewicz soaked up the works of abstract expressionism, the standout American art movement of the 1940s and 1950s. They loved its use of colour, albeit in a "free" form, very different to the patterns and geometry that came to define Op Art.

SHOWTIME IN NEW YORK

After Yale, Anuszkiewicz began to develop the style for which he is best known, abstract paintings that pulsate and glow with their arrangement of intense warm and cool colours and lines. Taking his work to New York galleries, he gradually gained momentum, having his first solo show in 1960 and being included the 1963 MoMA exhibition, The Americans. *Knowledge and Disappearance* (1961), which featured in the show, made use of multiple red and grey rectangles arranged to give the viewer the impression that they are staring, or falling, into a deep box.

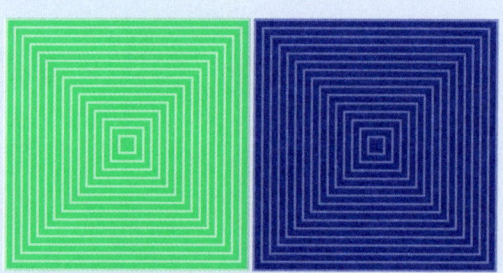

RICHARD ANUSZKIEWICZ

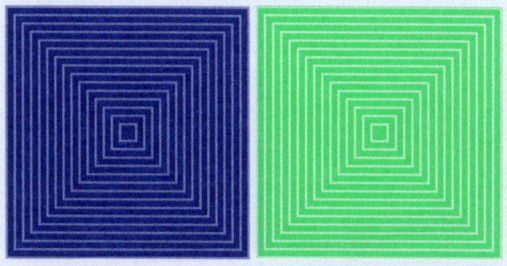

Anuszkiewicz's success in this
show led to his inclusion in MoMA's
The Responsive Eye exhibition (1965)
where *All Things Do Live in the Three* (1963)
was one of two pieces shown. Here,
small coloured dots of uniform size on
a coloured background are arranged in
overlapping geometric shapes of subtly
different colours that makes it at first
hard to read. The eye is then drawn into
the painting, which appears to vibrate
or hum, leaving a slightly unsettled
feeling or mild confusion about what
the viewer is seeing.

"People thought that
I always wanted to
shock the eye.
I didn't want to
shock the eye.
I wanted to use
colours together that
had never been used
together before."

RICHARD ANUSZKIEWICZ,
THE *NEW YORK TIMES*, 1985

FLUORESCENT COMPLEMENT

BY RICHARD ANUSZKIEWICZ, 1960

Location: MoMA, New York, USA

This artwork, one of Anuskiewicz's first in his new abstract style, was also his first painting to be sold in New York, contributing to his sudden fame and a solo show in the city. Its olive-green dots on a blue-green background, which become lighter towards the centre, play with our perception of colour and how this changes depending on the choice of adjacent colours.

HYPNOTIC TENDENCIES

Hailed by the *New York Times* as "one of the brightest stars in The Responsive Eye", Anuszkiewicz went on to be widely exhibited, including at the Venice Biennale, and won multiple awards. He developed a growing interest in the optical changes that occur when different colours are applied to the same geometric designs. He created several series of works in the later 1960s and 1970s, notably his *Sol* series, which featured paintings consisting of a central square or diamond of solid colour with a thick border of another bright contrasting colour, with nests of squares made of fine, lighter lines radiating outwards. His *Spectral* series played further on this idea with a single solid colour background overlaid with squares of coloured fine lines of a contrasting colour.

Accurately described as hypnotic and mesmerizing, these images created unstable visual effects where symmetrical imagery alternates between appearing to come towards the viewer and move away.

A LUMINOUS LEGACY

Deep Magenta Square (1978) is a similarly hypnotic piece showing a magenta square on a purple background with multiple lines of white light radiating out from behind it, giving an eclipse-like effect with the square covering a source of bright light. As with much of his work at this time, Anuszkiewicz repeated the same effect in different paintings using different colourways.

As time went on, Anuszkiewicz's work became even more mathematical in composition and he used masking tape to achieve his perfect lines. Through the 1980s his work achieved ever more luminosity and he also created geometric sculptures based on some of his 2D artworks. He died in 2020, a few days shy of his 90th birthday, leaving behind a rich body of work and a legacy of provoking an intense emotional response to colour in his dazzling paintings.

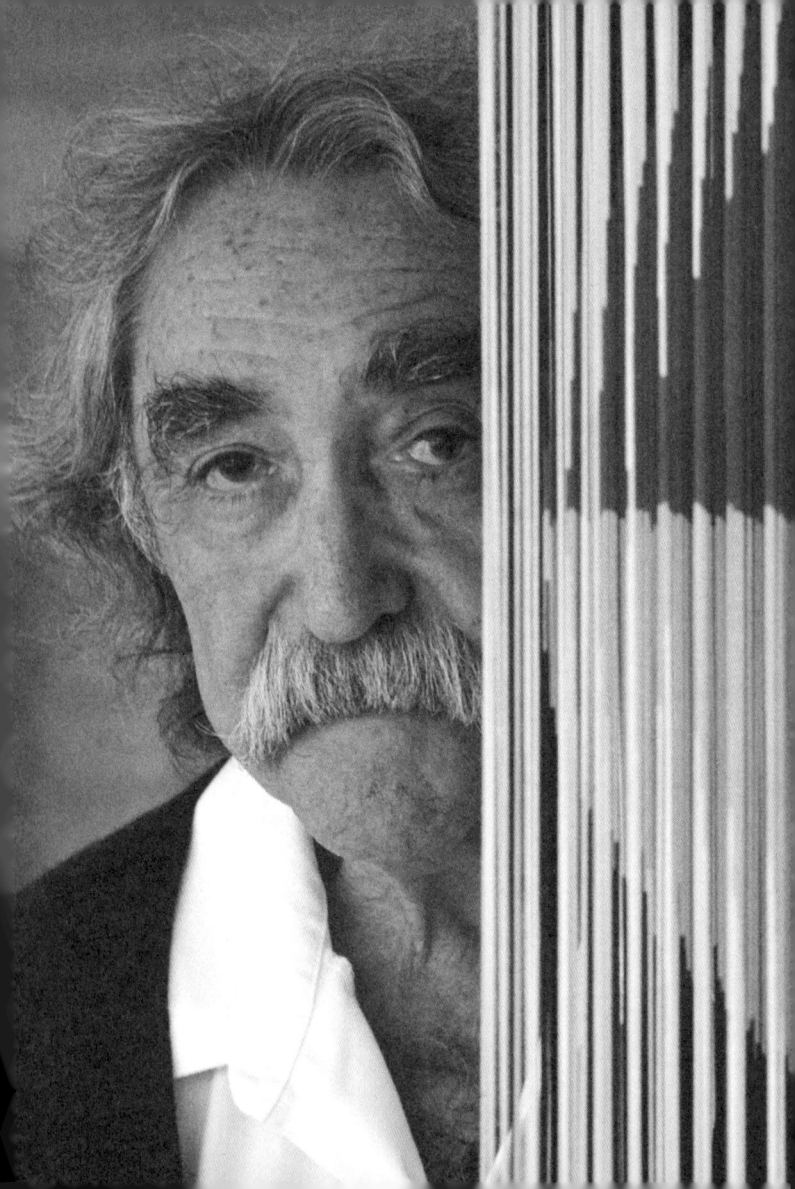

JESÚS RAFAEL SOTO

1923–2005

Place of birth/death:

Ciudad Bolívar, Venezuela/Paris, France

Key works:

Vibrations series (1950s)
Spirale (1955/59)
Untitled (1967)
Pénétrable (1967)
Escritura Hurtado (1975)

EARLY YEARS

Born in Venezuela in 1923, Jesús Rafael Soto is one of the op artists most associated with Op Art's adjacent movement, kinetic art. Much of his life's work explored the boundaries between painting and sculpture, and the perception of the viewer in this space.

The eldest of four children, Soto's artistic journey began aged 16, when he designed and painted posters for the cinemas in his home town to earn a little extra money for his family. His talent was noticed and he was given a scholarship to study fine art in the nation's capital, Caracas.

FIRST IMPRESSIONS

The art school's director introduced Soto to the post-impressionists and cubists and he was inspired by their exploration of form over realism and the idea of seeing through multiple viewpoints. Other influences at this time included the constructivist movement and suprematist artist Kazimir Malevich.

"What interests me is the transformation of matter. Taking an element, a line, a bit of wood or metal, and transforming it into pure light... transforming it into vibrations."

JESÚS RAFAEL SOTO,
THEARTSTORY.ORG

JESÚS RAFAEL SOTO

1923–2005

Place of birth/death:

Ciudad Bolívar, Venezuela/Paris, France

Key works:

Vibrations series (1950s)
Spirale (1955/59)
Untitled (1967)
Pénétrable (1967)
Escritura Hurtado (1975)

EARLY YEARS

Born in Venezuela in 1923, Jesús Rafael Soto is one of the op artists most associated with Op Art's adjacent movement, kinetic art. Much of his life's work explored the boundaries between painting and sculpture, and the perception of the viewer in this space.

The eldest of four children, Soto's artistic journey began aged 16, when he designed and painted posters for the cinemas in his home town to earn a little extra money for his family. His talent was noticed and he was given a scholarship to study fine art in the nation's capital, Caracas.

Completing his studies in 1947, he worked as director of an art school in Maracaibo for three years before moving to France and settling in Paris, where he spent the rest of his life. Here, his love of geometric abstraction really developed. Like other op artists, he greatly admired the work of Paul Klee and also Dutch artist Piet Mondrian, founder of neoplasticism, with his use of geometric lines and shapes and primary colours. Soto's early 1950s work clearly shows this influence.

"Artistic creation is a force which should preferably be directed towards the exploration of space, of the universe, of the infinite realities which surround us, but of which we are hardly conscious."

JESÚS RAFAEL SOTO, ARTNET.COM

SPIRALE

BY JESÚS RAFAEL SOTO, 1959

Location: Mildred Lane Kemper Art Museum, St Louis, USA

Blurring the boundaries between Op Art and kinetic art, 1959's *Spirale* presents a white spiral printed on Plexiglass mounted just in front of another sheet with a black spiral on it. As the viewer looks at the piece from different angles, the spirals intersect with each other giving a sense of energy, movement, shimmering and interference. Called the moiré effect, it's a technique Soto returned to repeatedly.

KINETIC MEETS OP

Soto joined several art groups in 1950s Paris, and met and befriended Victor Vasarely, among others. His work was shown in the 1955 exhibition, Le Mouvement, which is seen by many as the debut of kinetic art. This helped to put him on the map and led to his direct association with the kinetic art-Op Art movement. Other exhibitions followed, although he was still playing guitar at night in bars to support his young family.

Fascinated since childhood by the effects of sunlight in nature, his work explored the interplay of light, movement and perception, in both 2D paintings and 3D sculptures and installation works. Many of Soto's works from the late 1950s and 1960s that fall under the Op Art banner are untitled, including 1967's *Untitled*, which shows classic Op Art black and white painted lines and rectangles, evenly arranged to give the appearance of looking through a 3D blind.

IMMERSIVE EXPERIENCES

Throughout the 1960s, Soto's star continued to rise and he held major solo exhibitions as well as participating in group shows featuring Op Art, kinetic art, minimalism and more. He was also given prestigious commissions for large-scale public works of his kinetic installations worldwide, including the UNESCO headquarters in Paris in 1969. And in 1973, he created the Museo de Arte Moderno Jesús Soto with modernist architect Carlos Raúl Villanueva, in his hometown of Ciudad Bolívar in Venezuela where his work is shown alongside other kinetic and geometric artists.

JESÚS RAFAEL SOTO

Soto died in Paris, aged 81, in 2005, and is remembered for his energy-filled works that questioned perception, whether through 2D Op Art pieces or immersive kinetic pieces that left the observer literally surrounded by art.

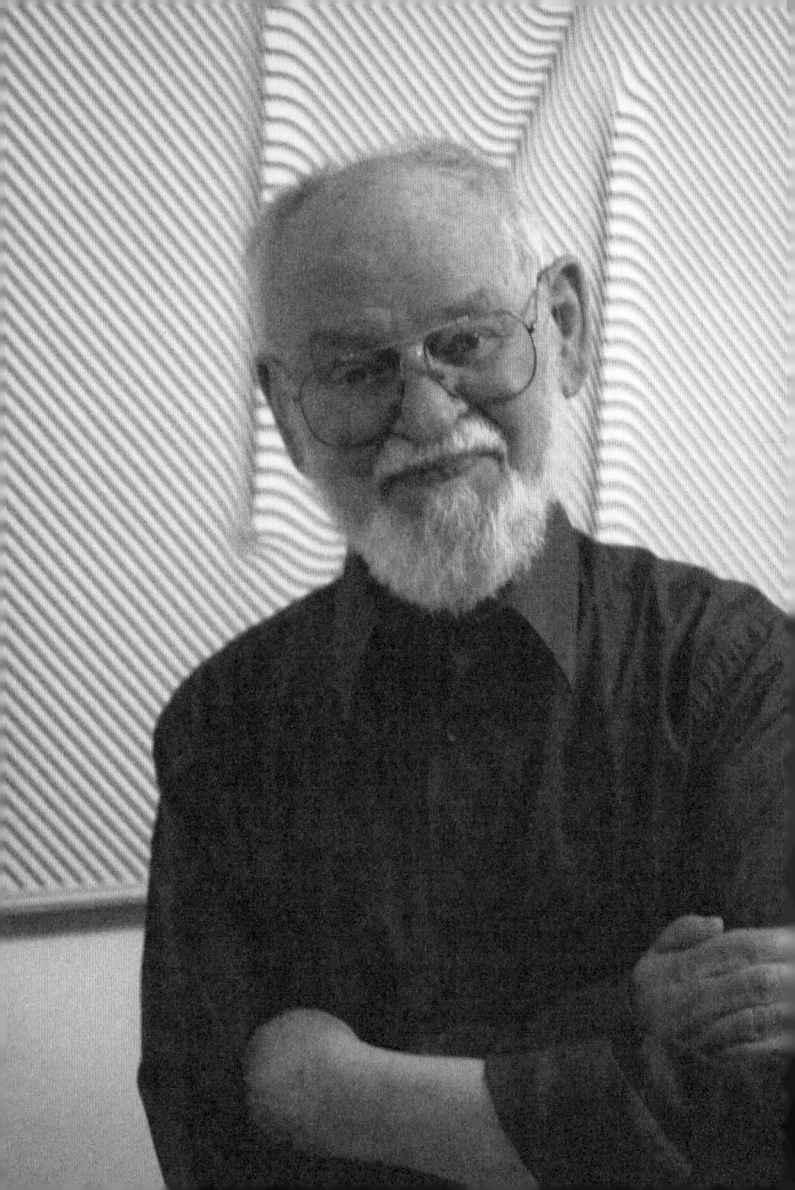

JULIAN STANCZAK

1928–2017

Place of birth/death:

Borownica, Poland/Ohio, USA

Key works:

Spring Colors (1957)
Walking Shadows (1962)
Belated Echo (1965)
Anywhere – Everywhere (1967)
Chromatic Fold, Acra Yellow (1970)

EARLY YEARS

Born in Poland in 1928, Julian Stanczak suffered extreme hardship in his early life when his family was sent to a Siberian labour camp in 1939. The dreadful conditions resulted in him losing the use of his dominant right arm and so he trained himself to write, draw and paint with his left.

Stanczak's family escaped the camp in 1941 and made their way overland to a refugee camp in Uganda where they stayed until relocating to London, England, in 1948. During his time in Africa, Stanczak practised his art skills under the tutelage of a fellow refugee, and drew inspiration from both his stunning natural surroundings and the geometric patterns of local textiles. In London, he studied illustration for two years before moving with his family to the United States, which he would make his home.

ABSTRACTED LINEAR PATTERNS

Stanczak went to the Cleveland Institute of Art and, in 1954, to Yale, where he roomed with fellow future op artist, Richard Anuszkiewicz, and studied under Josef Albers. It was here that he began working in a more abstract style and developed his interest in colour theory.

After Yale, Stanczak taught at the Art Academy of Cincinnati for seven years, while developing his own style, described as "abstracted linear pattern", and exhibiting where he could. In 1955, he won plaudits for his work in an exhibition of new art in Cleveland, but it wasn't until 1964, when it was spotted by influential New York gallery owner Martha Jackson, that his career really took off.

"My primary interest
is colour – the energy
of the different
wavelengths of
light and their
juxtapositions.
Colour is abstract,
universal – yet
personal and private
in experience."

"I found line – repeated line with its potent timing, its rising and falling rhythm – paralleling many aspects of daily life. From the point of action, line behaviour is distinct from colour; line activates the surface of the canvas more than a single flat colour."

JULIANSTANCZAK.COM

SHOW AND TELL

Martha Jackson invited Stanczak to
exhibit in New York and his 1964 show,
Optical Paintings, earned him favourable
comparisons with established op artist
Bridget Riley as well as becoming
the origin of the name of the Op Art
movement itself.

Stanczak's work also appeared in MoMA's
Op Art blockbuster, The Responsive Eye,
in 1965, after which his career went from
strength to strength. He exhibited widely,
both as a solo artist and part of a group,
and while also teaching at the Cleveland
Institute of Art, where he was professor of
painting from 1964–95.

CHROMATIC FOLD, ACRA YELLOW

BY JULIAN STANCZAK, 1970

The bright colours for which Stanczak is best known can be seen in the classic example of *Chromatic Fold, Acra Yellow* (1970), where overlapping geometric shapes of subtly different complementary colours sit on a background of fine, evenly spaced lines. The 3D effect produced makes it hard to identify the colours at first glance.

"If I take time to really look at what I'm seeing, there is no limit to the secrets unveiled."

JULIANSTANCZAK.COM

MONO OR COLOUR

Stanczak's work was described as showing "fields of narrow, vibrating stripes", which can be seen in early pieces, such as 1957's *Spring Colors*, where red, green and pink lines are arranged in stripes in asymmetrical shapes. The colours and their arrangement confuse the eye and produce a distinctly 3D effect.

Walking Shadows (1962) is a more classically Op Art monochrome, with black, white and grey lines on a darker background imitating the moving nature of shadows in a geometric style. *Anywhere – Everywhere* (1967) is another monochrome piece that shimmers like light on shiny metal, distorting the image as the eye tries to perceive it.

WHAT'S IN A NAME

A major figure in the Op Art movement, Stanczak's work is shown in many prestigious galleries around the world, and only grew in complexity even as Op Art fell from vogue. By the 1980s, he was often using more than 100 colour mixes in a single painting. Colour play remained at the heart of his work with parallel lines or grids of multiple squares often in evidence. Stanczak continued working until shortly before his death in 2017 and will always be remembered as the artist whose exhibition named the movement.

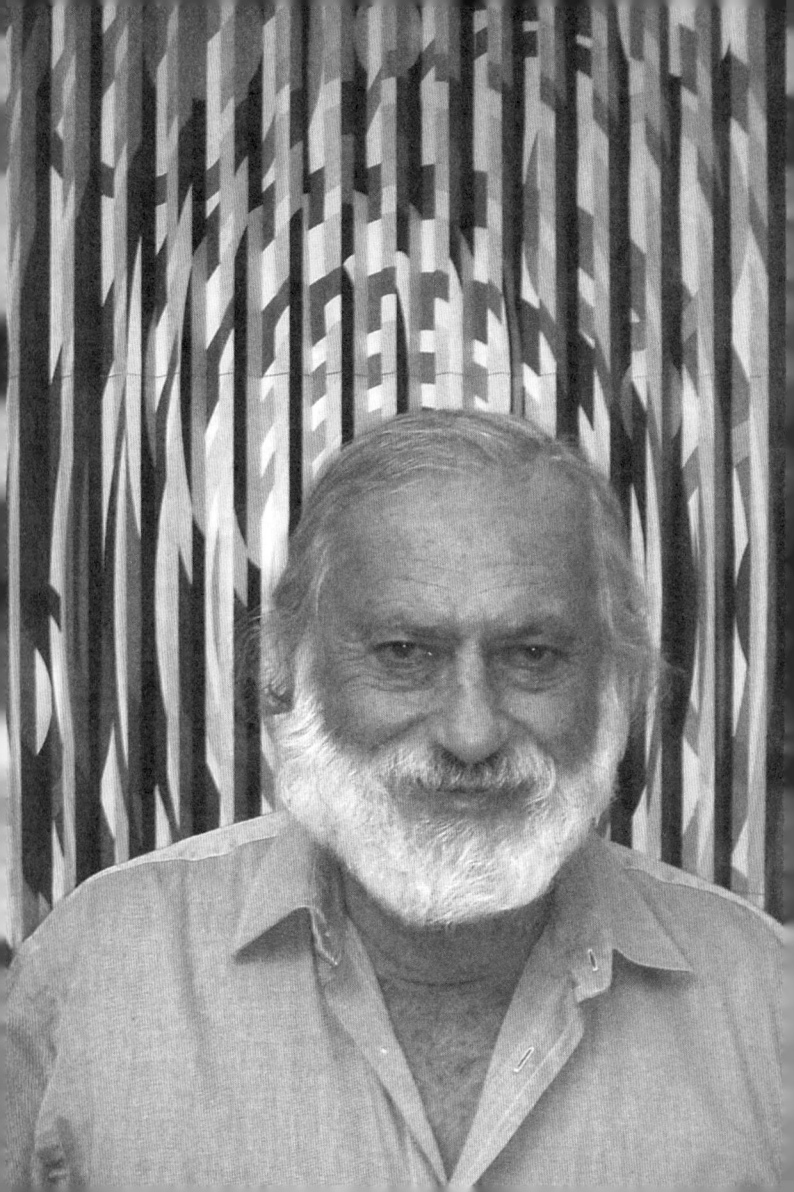

YAACOV AGAM

1928–

Place of birth:

Rishon LeTsiyon, Israel

Key works:

Double Metamorphosis III (1965)
Relief Rhythm (1966)
Three Times Three Interplay (1970–71)
The Thousand Gates (1972)
Visual Music Orchestration (1989)

EARLY YEARS

Yaacov Agam, the son of a Russian rabbi, grew up in an early Jewish settlement. Having learned to draw at an early age, and not beginning a formal schooling until he was 13, he eventually studied at the Bezalel School of Art in Jerusalem from 1947–48). In 1951 he travelled to Paris and in 1953, had his first one-man exhibition, Paintings in Movement, at the Craven Gallery.

An early pioneer of optical and kinetic art, Agam's body of work has since grown over the years to include paintings and 3D objects that include tactile elements, often with manipulable, sculptural properties.

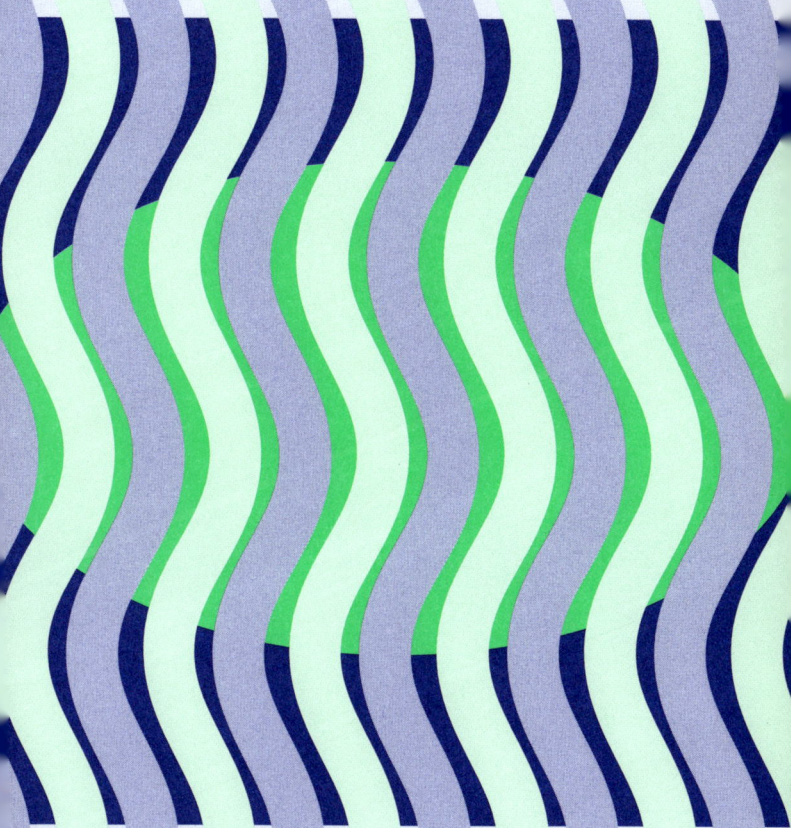

YAACOV AGAM

RELIEF RHYTHM

BY YAACOV AGAM, 1966

Crossing over between Op Art, kinetic art and sculpture, this work uses abstract geometric forms to engage the viewer in a multitude of possible compositions. The work thus appears to be in constant motion and a changing entity, transforming as the viewer moves around it or changes their viewing position.

"There are two distinct languages. There is the verbal, which separates people... and there is the visual that is understood by everybody."

YAACOV AGAM,
PARKWESTGALLERY.COM, 2017

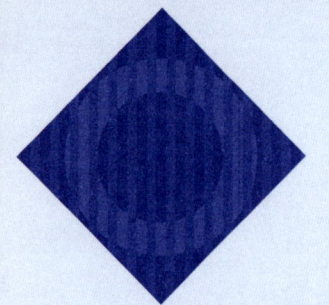

AGAMOGRAPHIC PRINTS

Agam is recognized for his work using a type of print known as an "Agamograph". Using a lenticular technique, it features a barrier-grid animation that presents radically different images, depending on the angle from which it is viewed.

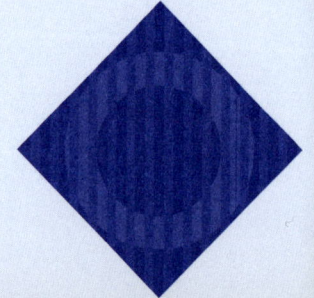

"My aim is to show what can be seen within the limits of possibility which exists in the midst of coming into being."

YAACOV AGAM,
HOMAGE TO AGAM: SOLOMON R.
GUGGENHEIM MUSEUM EXHIBITION,
1980

IN RETROSPECT

Agam has had numerous exhibitions and installations worldwide, both in a group and as a solo artist, including shows at the MoMA in New York, in St Louis, Paris, Dusseldorf, Jerusalem and more. In particular, his retrospective exhibition was held in Paris, at the Musée National d'Art Moderne in 1972, and at the Guggenheim Museum in New York City in 1980. His works are held in numerous museum collections, including the Museum of Modern Art and the Mildred Lane Kemper Art Museum.

THE WINNER TAKES ALL

Yaacov Agam designed and created the winner's trophy for the 1999 Eurovision Song Contest held in Jerusalem that year. The winners were Sweden, with their song 'Take Me To Your Heaven', performed by Charlotte Nilsson.

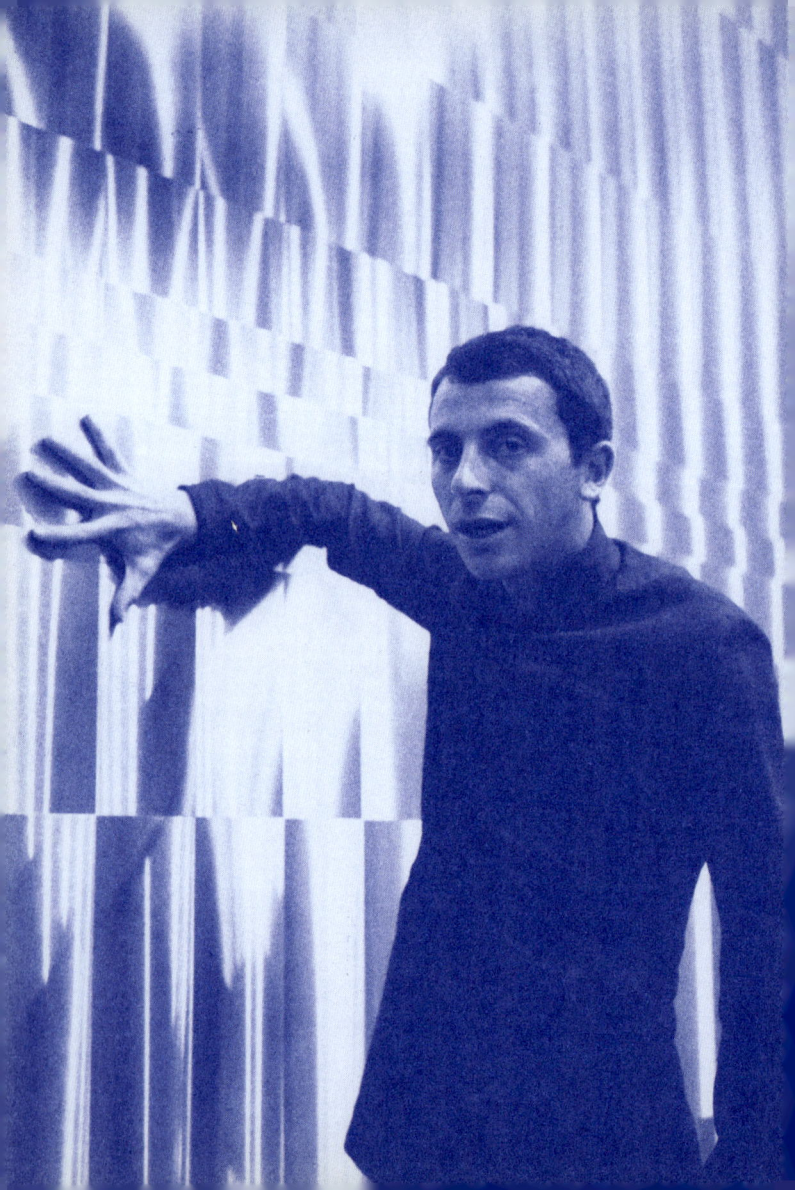

GETULIO ALVIANI

1939–2018

Place of birth/death:

Udine, Italy/Milan, Italy

Key works:

Wires series (1950s)
Tensione Structures series (1960s)
Vibrating Texture Surfaces series (1960s)
Reflection with Orthogonal Incidence (1967)
Graphic Texture Cube (1964–69)
Blue and Red Spirals (1968)

EARLY YEARS

Born in Udine, Italy, in 1939, op and kinetic artist Getulio Alviani showed an aptitude for art from an early age and enrolled at art school in Venice. To support himself, he worked for local architects and an electrical engineering firm, there developing an interest in design and construction using the latest technology. He enjoyed analyzing the technical production of new objects in detail and this, in turn, led to him adopting design-led approaches to his art.

Alviani was influenced by Bauhaus teachings and the constructivists' use of mechanical objects to inspire abstract structural forms. He took inspiration from the industrial materials around him and began to use steel and aluminium panels in his work. As with other op artists, he was interested in the nature of perception and experimented with what the viewer sees in his metallic pieces.

FINE WIRING

His first series, *Wires*, drew inspiration from aerial electrical wires and was praised for its dynamic and minimalist style. It is one of Alviani's most significant contributions to Op Art and kinetic art. Here, he used polished aluminium surfaces that were meticulously engraved with parallel lines, or "wires", creating a dynamic impression of movement.

Following on from *Wires*, Alviani gained significant recognition with his early 1960s *Vibrating Texture Surfaces*, a series of textured panels made from scratched and polished aluminium pieces in regular geometric patterns.

"I have two friends, who are the greatest friends I've ever had in life, I always have them with me, and they are the lens and the ruler. They have never betrayed me, they are always calm, safe and make no mistake."

GETULIO ALVIANI, INTERVIEW WITH HANS ULRICH OBRIST, *PROSPECTIVES*, 2015

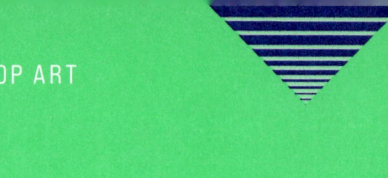

"In a split second,
I see everything,
and everything is
verifiable. One of my
passions is synthesis,
so it is obvious that
I love the eyes. For
me the eyes are
everything."

GETULIO ALVIANI, INTERVIEW WITH HANS
ULRICH OBRIST, *PROSPECTIVES*, 2015

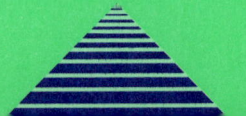

SURFACE WITH VIBRATING TEXTURE

BY GETULIO ALVIANI, 1964

Location: MoMA, New York, USA

This is a quintessential example of Alviani's treatment of fine aluminium. Inscribed parallel lines create a highly reflective, textured surface which results in a melange of shifting light, with pieces all the while seeming to vibrate and hum.

ON SHOW

Alviani's work was popular – he had his first solo show in 1961 and here met influential art critic and curator, Umbro Apollonio. By 1964, he was exhibiting at the Venice Biennale. He consorted with other well-known artists from a variety of modernist abstract movements in both Europe and the United States and was invited to participate in The Responsive Eye at MoMA in New York in 1965.

SCALING UP

In the later 1960s, Alviani produced large-scale installation pieces, some of which were displayed on the floor and designed to be walked over. *Reflection with Orthogonal Incidence* (1967) was a grid of ridged steel panels placed at right angles to each other to produce a black and white chequerboard effect. And his *Graphic Texture Cube* (1964–69), presented three sides of a cube covered in panels of silvery opalescent PVC woven in a lattice effect. Visitors were able to stand within the 10-foot (3-metre) high cube to gain the full effect of its disorientating walls.

AN EXPANSIVE APPROACH

Always innovating, Alviani also made abstract jewellery pieces, designed clothing – notably his 1964 Positivo-negativo dress with fashion designer Germana Marucelli – and worked on architectural projects. He wrote theories on art and studies on architecture, and was the recipient of several international art awards. In 1973, Jesús Rafael Soto invited Alviani to run his newly created

Jesús Soto Museum of Modern Art in Venezuela, where he helped bring together the work of op and kinetic artists worldwide.

Alviani died in Milan in 2018, but remains widely revered, not only as part of the Op Art and kinetic art movements, but as an art polymath and highly influential figure in late 20th-century art.

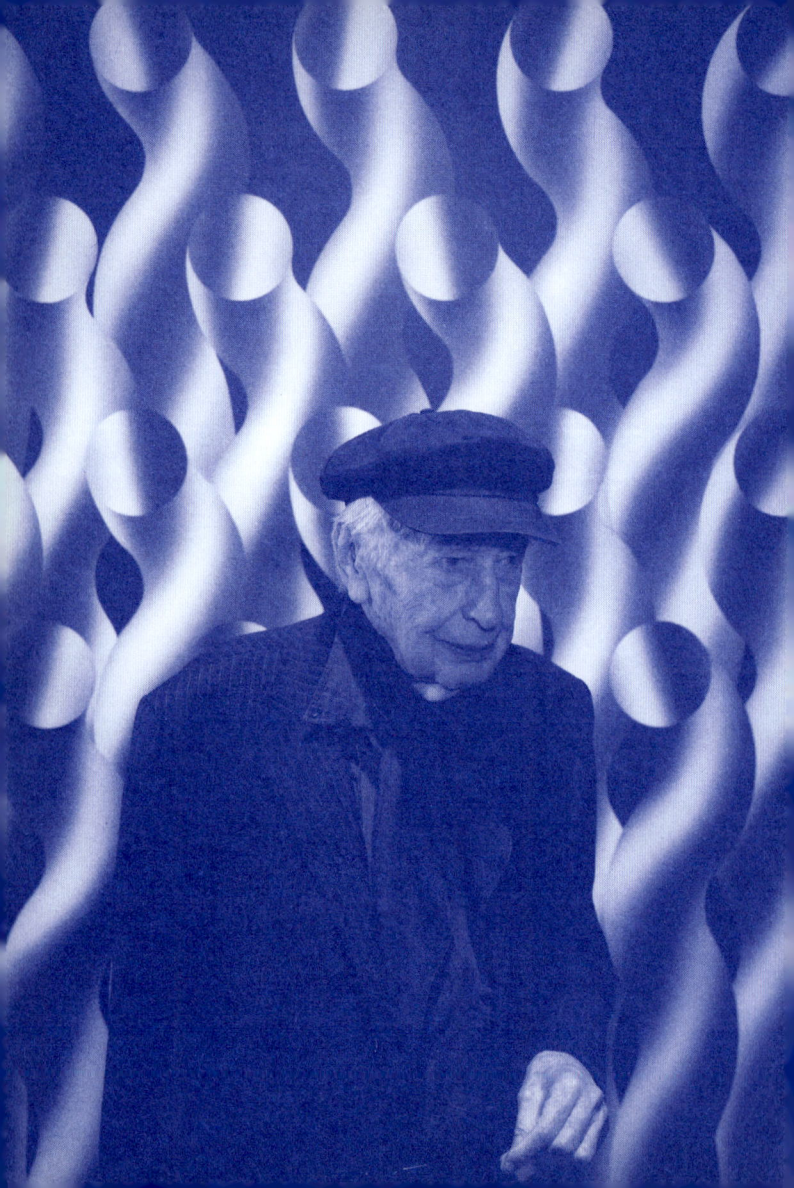

JULIO
LE PARC

1928–

Place of birth:

Palmira, Argentina

Key works:

Continual Mobile, Continual Light (1963)
Virtual Forms in Various Situations (1965)
Light in Movement (1962)
Cellule Avec Lumière en Vibration (1968)
Alchemy 175 and *216* (1991 and 1992)
Modulation 1160 (2004)
La Longue Marche (1974)

EARLY YEARS

Argentinian modernist, Julio
Le Parc, was born in Mendoza,
Argentina, in 1928. At the age of 13,
he moved to Buenos Aires with his
family and discovered a talent for
drawing. He took evening classes
at the School of Fine Arts, while
working during the day to support
himself, and later studied at the
Academy of Fine Arts in the city.
From the early 1950s onwards, Le
Parc took an interest in kinetic art,
researching ideas around movement
and the experience of the viewer
in his work.

"I wanted to leave aside sentimentality to allow accessibility to people who had no history, to involve them. I was attacking the static nature of artworks. More importantly, I was attacking the idea of the extraordinary artist."

JULIO LE PARC,
THE *INDEPENDENT*, 2014

GETTING ABSTRACTED

In 1957, Le Parc held his first exhibition, in São Paulo, Brazil, and in 1958, he received a grant to go to Paris. Here, he met up with fellow South American artists, Jesús Rafael Soto and Carlos Cruz-Diez, and together they became part of the young avant-garde art circles that included Victor Vasarely and other abstract artists. Le Parc counted Vasarely as one of his inspirations, along with Piet Mondrian and the constructivists, and his art reflected this.

GOING GEOMETRIC

Shortly after he arrived in Paris, in 1959 Le Parc produced a series of geometric abstract works, most in black and white but some in colour. These included *Tribute*, *Quantitative Sequences* and *Progressions in Lines and Color*, all of which prefigured Op Art in their illusions of movement and the way they involve the eye and its way of processing information.

GROUP WORK

In 1960, Le Parc became a founder member of the Groupe de Recherche d'Art Visuel (GRAV), a collective of 11 op-kinetic artists who believed that the notion of the solo artist was outdated and who focused heavily on the viewers' experience and interaction with their collective works. The group produced interactive labyrinths, including one for the third Paris Biennale in 1963, which invited visitors to walk through 20 experiences in different rooms. This early precursor to immersive art was popular but the group wasn't able to hold together and disbanded in 1968.

CONTINUAL MOBILE, CONTINUAL LIGHT

BY JULIO LE PARC, 1963

Location: Tate, London, England

In 1960, Le Parc made the first of his long-running *Continual Mobiles* series, introducing movement and light in works that he wanted to be seen in continuous motion. In this piece he used metal strips or squares, suspended in regular patterns on nylon strings in front of a plain background, with air currents providing continual movement. He developed this theme by exploring the use of artificial light, with reflected, projected or pulsating lights, to mesmerizing and disorientating effect.

"My pleasure was
to imagine all these
variations happening
over time, and my
calculations of
probability brought
me to consider
another situation:
unlimited duration."

JULIO LE PARC,
JULIO LE PARC 1959 EXHIBITION, THE
METROPOLITAN MUSEUM OF ART, 2019

GOING SOLO

Le Parc appeared in MoMA's landmark 1965 exhibition, The Responsive Eye, showing *Instability through Movement of the Spectator* (1962–64), painted wood and polished aluminium in a black wooden box that produced absorbing distorted images. As with other op artists, this exhibition boosted Le Parc's profile and the following year he had his first solo exhibition, also in New York, and won the Grand Prize in Painting at the Venice Biennale.

Le Parc continued to create Op Art and kinetic art in subsequent years, holding multiple major solo shows in every decade. Always at the heart of his work, however, is his desire to make accessible art and to have the viewer and their experience intrinsic to the piece.

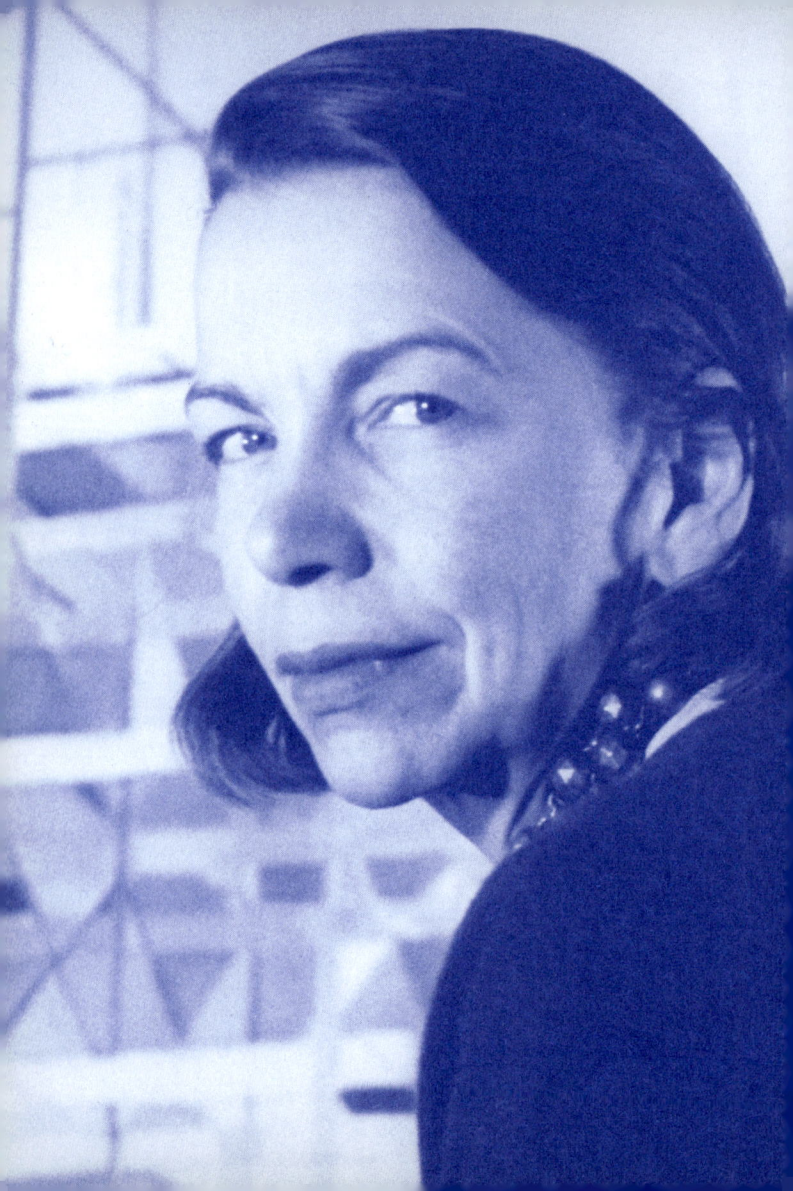

EDNA ANDRADE

1917–2008

Place of birth/death:

Portsmouth, Virginia, USA/
Philadelphia, Pennsylvania, USA

Key works:

Color Motion 4-64 (1964)
Turbo 1-65 (1965)
Radiant Ellipse 3-65 (1965)
Four Hot Planets (1965)
Space Frame - D (1966–67)
Night Sea (1977)

EARLY YEARS

Born in Virginia in 1917, Edna Andrade studied art in Philadelphia, first at the University of Pennsylvania and then at the Pennsylvania Academy of the Fine Arts. Travel in Europe after the Second World War introduced her to the Bauhaus movement and a wealth of modernist art, which was to influence her work and take her in the direction of geometric abstraction.

After working in graphics, and following her divorce, she went on to teach at the Philadelphia College of Art in 1960. At this point, she began to move towards purer studies of colour and abstract geometric form.

"Nature generates her rich variety of forms. She teaches me geometry and I borrow shapes and colours, symmetries, rhythms, and ratios from her."

EDNA ANDRADE,
'EDNA ANDRADE: THE GEOMETRY OF PERCEPTION' BY JOHN DORFMAN,
ART & ANTIQUES, 2019

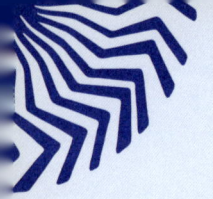

COLOURING IN

Fascinated with the overlap between science and art, and inspired by the geometric patterns she saw in nature, Andrade's work was a natural fit with the Op Art movement.

She'd studied colour theory and wanted to explore the way motion could be created in a painting by using repeating patterns and contrasting colours. *Color Motion 4-64* (1964) was one of Andrade's first key works, and it features a grid of four squares filled with chequerboard patterns that pulsate and bulge towards the viewer. A later work, *Turbo 1-65* (1965), created a mesmeric optical illusion with its rich colours and strong red and green stripes vibrating and moving under the viewer's gaze.

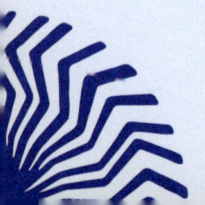

RADIANT ELLIPSE 3-65

BY EDNA ANDRADE, 1965

Location: Locks Gallery, Philadelphia, USA

This was one of a series of Op Art-style works painted in oils on linen, showing colourful circles within ovals within a square, and featuring strong, thick geometric lines within each shape in a cascade of pale orange, green, blue and grey. Almost like an eye looking out at the viewer, it plays with our perception as the shapes seem to move and rotate before us.

THE SHAPE OF THINGS TO COME

Andrade played widely with many Op Art ideas and her 1960s work is some of the most dizzying. Patterns, colour and geometry continued to form the core of her work in the 1970s and 1980s, but under the clear influence of the natural world. By the 1990s and 2000s, she had returned to a more realistic style, drawing and painting rock formations observed along the coast of Maine.

Based in Philadelphia, Andrade didn't yet have gallery representation in 1965, and didn't show at The Responsive Eye in New York, but she did benefit from the boost this exhibition gave to the Op Art movement. She had her first solo show in 1967, and her work only gained in popularity as she got older. Andrade's work is shown in major galleries worldwide, and she held two major retrospectives, in 1993 and 2003, before she died in Philadelphia, in 2008.

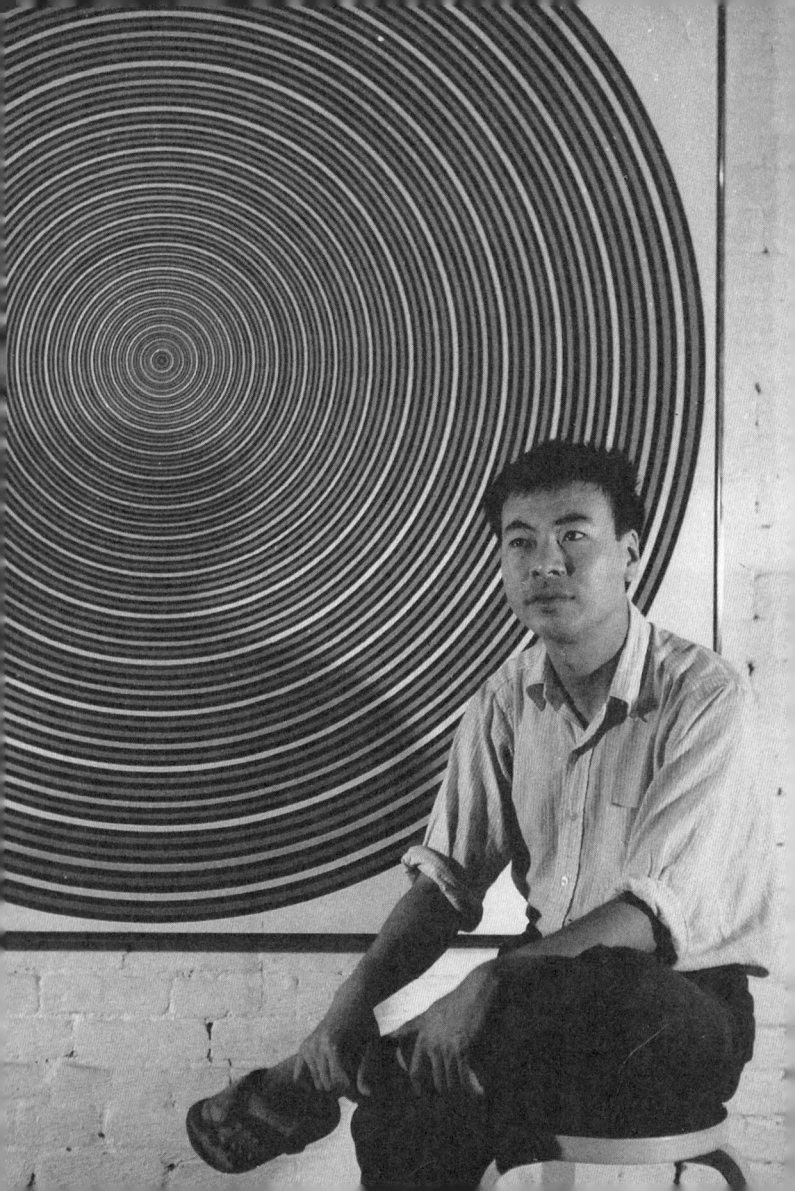

TADASKY
(TADASUKE KUWAYAMA)

1935–

Place of birth:

Nagoya, Japan

Key works:

A-101 (1964)
B-171 (1964)
B-181 (1964)
C-162 (1965)
C-200 (1965)
Untitled (various)

EARLY YEARS

Tadasky (Tadasuke Kuwayama) grew up in Nagoya, Japan, where his father was a well-known maker of Shinto shrines, and he has lived and worked in New York City and upstate New York since 1961. Originally he came to the USA on a scholarship to Cranbrook Academy of Art and Brooklyn Museum Art School in New York.

Exhibiting in MoMA's The Responsive Eye exhibition in 1965, he was a key figure in the early Op Art scene in the 1960s, with connections to the other artists of that movement, and with an abiding admiration for the Bauhaus group. He also became part of Jiro Yoshihara's Gutai group in Osaka, Japan in the early 1960s.

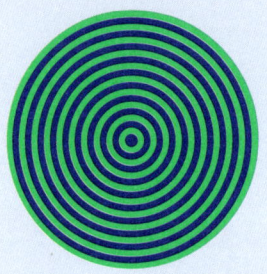

ROUND AND ROUND

Tadasky's signature works feature concentric circles, often in vibrant, contrasting colours. These mesmerizing pieces use optical effects to play with the viewer's perceptions of depth, movement and interaction. His work is noted for its mathematical precision, and the circular patterns create a pulsating energy, which are all key elements of the Op Art movement. Tadasky has exhibited in major galleries and museums, making him another successful member of the movement.

B-181

BY TADASKY, 1964

One of Tadasky's most important and widely recognized works today, this piece is a defining example of his contribution to Op Art. The precision of the circular lines and the way the colours interact creates a very physical response to the work. Making use of a repeated four-colour pattern, the work has a vibrancy and intensity that causes a flickering or pulsing effect, It exemplifies Tadasky's commitment to a more universal and non-verbal language through art.

"Looking at one of my paintings is for me like entering a traditional Shinto shrine. Because they are both so simple and symmetrical, the impact is very powerful."

TADASKY, INTERVIEW WITH JULIE KARABENICK, GEOFORM, 2013